Sexual Violence Research Roundtable

MEETING SUMMARY

Arlington, Virginia
September 8–9, 2011

National Institute of Justice
810 Seventh Street, NW
Washington, DC 20531

Office on Violence Against Women
145 N Street, NE
Washington, DC 20530

SEXUAL VIOLENCE RESEARCH ROUNDTABLE

Purpose and Background

The Office on Violence Against Women (OVW) and the National Institute of Justice (NIJ), both components of the United States Department of Justice, convened a roundtable discussion on research on sexual violence on September 8 and 9, 2011, in Arlington, Virginia. This roundtable built on two previous discussions, hosted by NIJ and OVW, respectively:

- On June 23 and 24, 2008, NIJ convened a Sexual Violence Research Workshop to take stock of current research on the criminal justice system response to sexual violence and to discuss ways to further develop research and disseminate findings to practitioners and policymakers. Among the topics that participants discussed were the application of forensic science to the investigation and prosecution of sexual assault and the multidisciplinary response to sexual assault. The discussion yielded valuable information that has informed NIJ's and other federal agencies' efforts to improve knowledge and practice related to the criminal justice system's handling of sexual assault cases.

- On October 27 and 28, 2010, OVW, in partnership with the White House Council on Women and Girls and Lynn Rosenthal, White House Advisor on Violence Against Women, convened a roundtable to discuss barriers to advancing the issue of sexual violence and to explore ways to overcome those barriers. A priority that emerged from the discussion is the need for more relevant, practitioner-informed research on sexual violence related to topics including but not limited to: incidence, prevalence, and reporting rates; victim recovery; law enforcement response; and prosecution and adjudication of sex crimes. OVW has since been working collaboratively with NIJ, the Bureau of Justice Statistics (BJS), and the Office for Victims of Crime (OVC) to bring this call from the field to fruition.

The September 2011 roundtable brought together experts on sexual violence, representing fields including research and academia, victim advocacy, law enforcement, prosecution, the judiciary, and health care; as well as several survivors of sexual violence whose voices kept victims' experiences at the center of the discussion. Over the course of the meeting, participants identified new and emerging priorities for research on the criminal justice system's response to sexual assault and generated ideas for bridging the gap between research and practice.

Morning Session

Welcome

Honorable Susan B. Carbon, Director, Office on Violence Against Women (OVW)

Director Carbon opened the roundtable by noting an important anniversary coming up on September 13—the 17th anniversary of the passage of the historic Violence Against Women Act (VAWA). She commented on how "deeply committed" the Obama Administration is to the issue of violence against women, and she saluted Vice President Biden for pressing hard for this legislation almost two decades ago as a senator and for advancing policies in this area now in the White House. She stated that the law "has transformed our nation's response to the tragic crimes of domestic violence, sexual assault, stalking, and dating violence. Hundreds of thousands of victims have benefitted, and their lives have been forever changed because of the resolve and commitment to end violence demonstrated not only by Congress, but by all of those who have worked so hard over the past 17 years to implement this legislation in their crisis centers, police departments, emergency rooms, prosecutors' offices, courtrooms, and communities. We are a different country than we were 17 years ago."

Director Carbon stressed the need to "maintain our vigilance" and uphold the responsibility of ensuring that friends, family, colleagues, communities, strangers, and people from all walks of life in this country work to broaden efforts to end violence against women, children, and men. She added that too many continue to be victimized, and as new professionals and volunteers enter the field, we need to ensure that they have access to the best practices and training as we are faced with new challenges and tools of abuse.

For the first time in the history of OVW, Director Carbon noted, there is a grant program that focuses primarily on the prevention of sexual assault, domestic violence, dating violence, and stalking by acknowledging the critical role men and boys play in addressing these issues. Along with the program's focus on the creation of public education campaigns through the work of community-based organizations in collaboration with local community partners, the result has been great interest and excitement from the field and potential applicants. Last month, OVW held its first New Grantee Orientation for OVW's *Engaging Men* grantees, and 23 sites were awarded in this first round, she reported. "With men as partners in this work," she said, "we have the potential to reach men and boys in new and creative ways, implementing programs most relevant to them and their communities."

Director Carbon then announced that hosting this week's Sexual Violence Research Roundtable marks an important step forward with the National Institute of Justice (NIJ), one of OVW's Department of Justice colleagues. She explained that the idea for this roundtable grew out of October 2010's first-ever White House Roundtable on Sexual Violence in the United States, noting that this partnership with NIJ brings together an extraordinary group of practitioners (representing medicine and health care, law enforcement, the judiciary, prosecution, and advocacy communities) along with some of the finest researchers in the country. "As we celebrate the 17th Anniversary of VAWA," she continued, "this moment also is important because we are working on the third reauthorization for this law." In addition to this meeting, OVW will later in the week announce the awards for its new Sexual Assault Demonstration Initiative (SADI). In early October, OVW will be hosting the National Summit on Campus Safety for College and University Presidents, which will bring in school presidents from around the country to discuss sexual assault and domestic violence on their campuses and how as key leaders they can lead their institutions in ending these crimes. Director Carbon then introduced Dr. John H. Laub, Director of NIJ.

John H. Laub, Ph.D., Director, National Institute of Justice

Dr. Laub thanked Director Carbon for convening the roundtable discussion. He said he was grateful for being able to partner with colleagues at OVW, the Bureau of Justice Statistics (BJS), and the Centers for Disease Control and Prevention (CDC) in formulating ways to enhance research and data collection relating to sexual violence.

As NIJ is the research, development, and evaluation arm of the U.S. Department of Justice, Dr. Laub said, one of his service goals in aiding those who help victims of sexual violence is to disseminate research findings that can be easily used and understood by those who put this research into practice. He stressed that at NIJ, the staff is committed to a concept he calls "translational criminology—preventing and reducing crime in our communities by translating scientific research into policy and practice. The heart of this concept," he explained, "is that by translating research evidence into sound crime policies and practices, NIJ will form a bridge between the work of research and the real-life challenges of fighting crime and enhancing justice." Dr. Laub stated that this roundtable is an important part of these translational efforts, and NIJ will use the information gathered to address gaps in the research on sexual violence response and criminal justice reform. "Our goal is to figure out what kind of research is necessary to encourage sexual violence victims to participate with the criminal justice system and maintain confidence that the system will indeed address their needs," Dr. Laub said.

Dr. Laub encouraged the meeting participants—researchers and practitioners alike—to exchange ideas and become familiar with each other, and, particularly, for the researchers to listen to the research needs expressed by practitioners in the audience. He also encouraged participants to apply for funding under next year's solicitation on researcher–practitioner partnerships. "We need more partnerships among researchers and practitioners," he said, "especially when it comes to addressing the problem of sexual violence."

Dr. Laub then acknowledged the roundtable coordination efforts of Bernard (Bernie) Auchter, an NIJ senior social science analyst of 35 years, and Virginia (Ginger) Baran, program specialist at OVW.

This document is intended to reflect the conversation among roundtable participants and does not necessarily reflect the opinions of the United States Department of Justice.

Icebreaker Exercise (Introduction of Attendees)

Following opening remarks, participants responded to statements they read from randomly selected slips of paper. They were asked to discuss how the statements they drew relate to their work. A sample of those statements are below accompanied by some of the participants' responses.

> Only one in five adult women report their rape to the police. About half of the women raped as adults who had contact with police and about half who had contact with the courts were satisfied with their treatment. (*Tjaden, P. & Thoennes, N. (2006).* Extent, nature, and consequences of rape victimization: Findings from the National Violence Against Women Survey. *Special Report. Washington, D.C.: National Institute of Justice and the Centers for Disease Control and Prevention.*)

One participant, a rape survivor, said she had a "wonderful" experience with the police officers who interviewed her after she was threatened, attacked, and assaulted by her husband. However, she said she received "horrible" treatment from health care workers who had no idea what to do even though they were charged with examining and caring for her after the assault. She went on to note that, overall, the experience was positive because her husband was convicted and she rebuilt her life. In her view, more women would be likely to report rape and pursue prosecution if they were treated from the outset in an understanding and caring way by law enforcement, health care practitioners, and other first responders.

Another participant noted that he was an emergency room doctor in the 1970s and that the intervening 40 years have produced changes in technology and forensic tools that now allow law enforcement to find, identify, and prosecute rapists. "This is a very interesting research area that I am proud to be a part of," he said.

> 17.6 percent of women in the United States have survived a completed or attempted rape. *(Findings from the National Violence Against Women Survey, November 2000)*

One participant said that this number shows how truly prevalent rape is and raises a simple question: "What are we going to do about it? The dirty little secret here is case attrition," the commenter said. Under this process, only a portion of offenses reported to police are eventually criminally prosecuted, and at each key decision-making point, the number of cases deemed worthy of official attention is reduced, with some cases carried forward for additional processing while others are no longer pursued to prosecution.

> I know it wasn't rape-rape. It was something else but I don't believe it was rape-rape. (Whoopi Goldberg on the charges against film director Roman Polanski for sexually assaulting a teenager in the 1970s.)

One participant, who disclosed that she is a survivor of sexual abuse, responded that this type of statement shows how prevalent the myths and misconceptions are surrounding sexual assault. "How do we women expect anyone else to know what rape is when we don't know what it is?" she asked.

Another participant urged colleagues in the field to break through the misconceptions, obtain the relevant data, analyze the data, and get the data out to police and prosecutors so that it is useful. "We cannot simply cherry-pick the data," he said.

> These young men will have to deal with this for the rest of their lives. (A woman in Cleveland, Texas, speaking in response to news that 18 men and boys raped an 11-year-old girl.)

All of the meeting participants expressed outrage upon hearing this statement. Several participants explained how this comment reflects the tendency to blame victims of sexual violence and make excuses for perpetrators.

> "The number of rape cases in Baltimore has dropped nearly 80 percent since 1992, a period in which rape cases declined by 8 percent nationally. Meanwhile, the proportion of rape reports deemed unfounded has increased fivefold since the late 1990s." (*Baltimore Sun, June 28, 2010*).

This comment clearly shows how critical it is to look at the organization that produces the statistic, one commenter said. In his view, it showed that there is a clear problem with the ways in which rape incidents are being counted (and *not* counted).

> Rape is the only crime in which the victim becomes the accused. (*Author and criminologist Freda Adler*)

Participants explained that this quote captures one reason why so many victims of sexual violence do not report their assaults, as they anticipate being blamed by police and prosecutors for the violence they endured. Another said the statement crystallizes the fact that often a victim is labeled a liar from the outset.

"It's also possible that she was sexually assaulted in every which way but rape. Yes, almost as bad, but still not as bad as rape." (*A Village Voice blogger in response to hearing that CBS reporter Lara Logan was sexually assaulted by a crowd of 200 to 300 men in Egypt.*)

One participant found this statement particularly troublesome, pointing out that it originates in the fact that society is "all over the place" in trying to define rape.

Another participant pointed to the rigid expression of "rape" under the FBI's Uniform Crime Reporting Program, which defines the offense as "carnal knowledge of a female forcibly and against her will." "Perhaps if this definition is broadened, so will people's idea of what rape is," she said. (Note: *In October 2011 the FBI stated plans to update the definition of rape that it has been using since the 1920s. The new definition, announced in January 2012 by United States Attorney General Eric Holder, is: "the penetration, no matter how slight, of the vagina or anus with any body part or object, or oral penetration by a sex organ of another person, without the consent of the victim." The new definition includes any gender of victim and perpetrator, and recognizes that rape with an object is in fact rape. This definition also accounts for rapes in which the victim is unable to give consent because of temporary or permanent mental or physical incapacity.*)

> Homeless women are far more likely to experience violence of all sorts than American women in general, ranging from two to four times more likely, depending on the violence type. Approximately one homeless woman in four is homeless mainly because of her experiences with violence. (Jasinski, J., Wesely, J., Mustaine, E., & Wright, J. (2005). *The experience of violence in the lives of homeless women, Final report*. Washington, DC: National Institute of Justice.)

One participant noted that this statement speaks to the broader problem of underreporting and to the greater risk faced by those who are marginalized. Poverty and lack of shelter are factors that make homeless women more vulnerable to sexual violence, the commenter said.

> In the current study, 81.6% of the survivors had previously disclosed the assault, supporting a growing body of literature that suggests that most survivors tell at least one person about the assault. (Ahrens, Cabral, & Abeling, 2009)

A participant explained that this research finding demonstrates the importance of supportive responses to survivors' disclosures.

> "Deliberate misuse of data by those who deny the prevalence of rape in our culture, careless use of data by rape activists, and inconsistent and confusing research reports have contributed to the common perception that a fake rape epidemic or crisis has been created." (TK Logan's white paper, *The Use (and*

This document is intended to reflect the conversation among roundtable participants and does not necessarily reflect the opinions of the United States Department of Justice.

February 2012 | Page 7 of 26

Misuse) of Data on Rape: Restoring Sexual Assault to the National Agenda,
prepared for the CounterQuo Conference October 17-19, 2008, p. 2.)

One participant gave an example of the inconsistencies in rape data in noting that in some communities (e.g., American Indian), the prevalence of sexual assault is even more staggering than in the population at large.

After the "icebreaker" session, participants were asked to consider over the next day and a half what research is urgently needed, and how best to disseminate research results to practitioners and the public.

Panel on Where We Stand: Statistics and Research on Sexual Violence

James P. Lynch, Ph.D., Director and Shannan Catalano, Ph.D., Statistician, Bureau of Justice Statistics

Dr. Lynch presented the following findings of the National Crime Victimization Survey (NCVS):

- ► Respectively, from 1993 to 2000 and from 2001 to 2009, the percentage of rapes and sexual assaults reported to police over time increased from below 30 percent to just below 40 percent.

- ► Sexual assaults and rapes reported to police in cases involving "intimates" increased from just over 20 percent (1993–2000) to well over 40 percent (2001–2009).

- ► "It's not important" is cited less often as a reason for not reporting sexual assault and rape to police during the 2001-2009 reporting period than during the 1993-2000 reporting period.

- ► From 2001 to 2009, police ineffectiveness and fear of reprisal were cited much more often than during the earlier reporting period as reasons for not reporting sexual assault and rape to police.

- ► From 2001 to 2009, police, when notified, took reports and searched for/took evidence much more often than they did during the 1993–2000 period. However, there was not a comparable increase in the number of arrests.

To Dr. Lynch, these data are clearly important in showing that sexual violence committed by "intimates" is no longer as underreported as in years past. Still, he said that fear of reprisal is a major concern of victims and one of the plaguing reasons that many cases go unprosecuted. The fact that the number of arrests remains flat in recent years is also a big concern, Dr. Lynch said. He said BJS would release a larger report on the NCVS in about two months.

Howard N. Snyder, Ph.D., Deputy Director, Bureau of Justice Statistics

Dr. Snyder presented a slide show that revealed the following important data from the FBI's National Incident Based Reporting System (NIBRS) for the period 2006–2008.

- ► Four of 10 (39 percent) violent sexual assaults known to law enforcement were forcible rapes.

- ► Two-thirds (65 percent) of victims of violent sexual assaults reported to law enforcement were under age 18, and one-third (31 percent) were under age 12.

- ► Females had their highest rate of sexual victimization at age 15.

- ► Males had their highest rate of sexual victimization at age 6.

This document is intended to reflect the conversation among roundtable participants and does not necessarily reflect the opinions of the United States Department of Justice.

- Violent sexual assault victimization rates were higher for blacks than whites in most age groups.

- Violent sexual assaults were most likely to occur from 8:00 a.m. to 9:00 a.m., noon to 1:00 p.m., and 3:00 p.m. to 4:00 p.m.—and to occur in a residence.

- Children under 12 were most likely to be assaulted from 8:00 a.m. to 9:00 a.m. and noon to 1:00 p.m.

- Juveniles ages 12–17 were most likely assaulted from noon to 1:00 p.m. and 3:00 p.m. to 4:00 p.m.

- Young adults ages 18–24 and adults ranging in age from 25 – 34 were most likely assaulted from 1:00 a.m. to 3:00 a.m.

- Adults ages 35 and older were most likely to be assaulted from 10:00 p.m. to 1:00 a.m.

Dr. Snyder noted that, for children, the ages for victimization drop after age 5 and peak at 14. This evidence indicates that children become less vulnerable to assault when they start to attend school, he said. The peak victimization for males at age 6 is very troublesome, as is the fact that African American women have a 50 percent higher risk than whites of being victims, Dr. Snyder said. Another figure that should give us all pause, he said, is that 71% of all sexual assaults occur in a residence. The analysis shows that rarely are perpetrators strangers to their victims. For example, less than 1% of victims under age 18 are victimized by stangers. He concluded by noting that a full report would be released in about two months.

Kathleen C. Basile, Ph.D., Lead Behavioral Scientist, National Center for Injury Prevention and Control (NCIPC), Centers for Disease Control and Prevention

Dr. Basile set forth a timeline of key points in the history of CDC's role in sexual violence prevention, beginning in 1994 with the first CDC-funded research grant on sexual violence. It was a decade of continued development that included the establishment of the National Sexual Violence Resource Center in 2001, the publication of *Sexual Violence and Surveillance: Uniform Definitions and Recommended Data Elements* in 2002, and the first optional sexual violence module in CDC's Behavioral Risk Factor Surveillance System (BRFSS) in 2005.

Dr. Basile noted that CDC's role has continued in recent years with: the National Intimate Partner and Sexual Violence Survey (NISVS) Pilot Test in 2007; the funding of research examining links between bullying and sexual violence in middle school in 2007 (3 years; $900,000); two evaluation studies of sexual violence prevention strategies in 2009 (3 years; $3.1 million); NISVS in the field for the first year of data collection in 2010; a meeting of an expert panel to suggest ways to update and reconcile CDC's Sexual Violence (SV) and Intimate Partner Violence (IPV) Definitions in 2010; and the upcoming release of the first NISVS report (2010 data).

Dr. Basile identified the NCIPC's sexual violence "Tier 1" research priorities as:

- ▶ Surveillance methods for sexual violence victimization and perpetration.

- ▶ Etiology of sexual violence perpetration.

- ▶ Linkages among sexual violence types, other types of violence, and other risk behaviors.

- ▶ Role of disparities.

- ▶ Efficacy and effectiveness trials for perpetration programs across all levels of social ecology.

- ▶ Efficacy and effectiveness trials of sexual violence programs and other violence programs.

In her SV definitions update, Dr. Basile noted that the 2010 expert panel sought feedback on updating and reconciling sexual violence and intimate partner violence definitions, and that currently the definitions are being edited so they can be shared with the panel and external reviewers. She reported that two of the eight key issues that the 2010 panel considered were sexual violence-related: how to incorporate sexual coercion and sexual harassment, and whether or not to use the language "completed sexual act."

The goals of NISVS, Dr. Basile said, are:

- ▶ To provide an ongoing source of detailed data to monitor the magnitude and characteristics of IPV, SV, and stalking in the United States.

- ▶ To increase our understanding of the nature, context, severity, and consequences of violence against women and men in the United States.

- ▶ To develop feasible approaches for monitoring IPV, SV, and stalking at the state and national level.

Dr. Basile reported that NISVS content comprises:

- ▶ Sexual Violence by Any Perpetrator
  - – Rape (completed, attempted, alcohol-/drug-facilitated)
  - – Being made to penetrate someone
  - – Sexual coercion
  - – Unwanted sexual contact
  - – Non-touch unwanted sexual experiences

- ▶ Stalking by Any Perpetrator

- ▶ Intimate Partner and Dating Violence
  - – Physical aggression

- Psychological aggression (expressive and coercive control and entrapment)
- Sexual violence
- Stalking

The NISVS model:

- ► Considers sexual violence over the lifespan:
  - Child sexual abuse
  - SV in dating context
  - Rape and other SV in marriage
  - SV of the elderly
- ► Examines numerous forms of SV
- ► Examines all victimization by the same perpetrator
- ► Considers SV in IPV context:
  - Co-occurrence and overlap of SV with other types of IPV;
  - Cumulative impact of all types of IPV by the same perpetrator.

The NISVS survey design further encompasses:

- ► Demographic and relationship information for individual perpetrators
- ► Patterns of violence
  - Forms of violence experienced
  - Duration
  - Frequency (12 months, lifetime)
- ► Impact of violence committed by individual perpetrators

The NISVS also measures impacts of violence such as:

- ► Concern for safety
- ► Fear
- ► Physical injuries
- ► Posttraumatic Stress Disorder symptoms
- ► Missed days of school/work
- ► Need for services

Dr. Basile further noted that NISVS asks:

- ► Did you ever need any of the following ...
  - Medical care?
  - Housing services?

- Community services?
- Victim's advocate services?
- Legal services?

▶ Were you able to get the services you needed?

▶ Which services were you not able to get?

▶ Why were you not able to get the assistance that you needed?

Dr. Basile explained that NISVS is different from previous surveys which have:

▶ Primarily been conducted within the context of crime or public safety (NCVS, NVAWS).

▶ Covered selected populations (e.g., schools, colleges, individual states).

▶ Included a small number of questions (YRBS, BRFSS, ICARIS-2).

▶ Not gathered national and state-level data at the same time.

Continuing, Dr. Basile described another study that examined SV victimization experienced by women of three racial/ethnic groups—African American, Hispanic, and American Indian/Alaska Native. This study included face-to-face interviews, provides detailed information on victimization episodes (vaginal, oral, or anal sex; unwanted touching and non-contact experiences), and examines numerous tactics for violence. The NISVS findings for these subgroups will be presented in three user-friendly reports.

Bethany L. Backes, Social Science Analyst, National Institute of Justice

Bethany L. Backes, NIJ social science analyst, then presented an overview of how NIJ determines a research agenda and develops proposal requests from year to year. She said that various factors like staff turnover and funding limitations come into play, but that NIJ tries to be consistent in ensuring a well-rounded approach to the research agenda. Various NIJ offices collaborate to minimize duplication and ensure that the necessary expertise is included to develop research priorities. This is followed by, she said, outreach and information gathering. NIJ staff review existing and past projects and remain current on research, practice and policy literature. Ms. Backes cited examples of work completed in NIJ's sexual violence portfolio over the past several years. Projects have been completed in the following areas:

▶ Criminal justice system response

▶ Sexual Assault Nurse Examiner (SANE)/Sexual Assault Response Team (SART)

▶ Forensics

▶ Incidence/prevalence

▶ Campus

This document is intended to reflect the conversation among roundtable participants and does not necessarily reflect the opinions of the United States Department of Justice.

- Diverse communities
- Sex offenders
- Sexual assault within the context of IPV
- Prevention and intervention
- Risk and protective factors
- Data systems and measurement

She also noted that the 2008 NIJ Sexual Violence Workshop looked at the criminal justice system (CJS) response, forensic science evidence, and the impact of SANE programs and SARTs, and she cited three noteworthy projects that NIJ recently funded, focusing on such issues as untested sexual assault kits, timeframe for evidence collection after sexual assault, and the development of a practitioner toolkit for evaluating Sexual Assault Nurse Examiner (SANE) programs. The abstracts for each of these projects can be found in the NIJ Violence Against Women Compendium – http://nij.gov/nij/pubs-sum/vaw-compendium.htm.

Ms. Backes encouraged more researcher–practitioner partnerships and stressed the need to have knowledge disseminated across disciplines. She highlighted the need for building a cumulative knowledge base while balancing science with the needs of the field.

Statistics and Data on Sexual Violence

TK Logan, Ph.D., Professor, University of Kentucky

Professor TK Logan of the University of Kentucky addressed gaps in literature. "The more I read, the more I don't know about sexual violence," she remarked. She observed that many papers fail to define "sexual violence," "sexual coercion," and related terms, and many also fail to explain the methodology used. Inconsistent labels for perpetrators is another common problem in research, as terms like "stranger," "intimate," and "date" do not have concrete definitions.

Thus, the terms used in sexual violence research studies must be clearly defined and the measures clearly articulated. Further, definitions may change over time for different generations. More attention to these basic factors must be incorporated into research.

Another gap in the research is the lack of context of sexual violence, particularly for partner violence. Many studies simply ask for a yes or no answer to questions about lifetime experience of sexual violence, or victimization since age 14, or just within the past year. However, a yes/no response is not enough. We must begin to better understand the context of the sexual assaults.

Professor Logan noted that the most powerful statements are those that provide a context for sexual assault by detailing frequency, severity, and duration of perpetrator conduct. Isolated statistics on the frequency of sexual assault do not capture the severity of these crimes, and lack of context is a barrier to better criminal justice responses. She said that it is time to break the silence around the context of sexual violence, particularly partner sexual violence and we can only do that by understanding and measuring the context. Using yes/no as the only or principal way to describe rape is not good enough.

Dean Kilpatrick, Ph.D., Distinguished University Professor of Clinical Psychology, Medical University of South Carolina

Dr. Kilpatrick, clinical psychology professor at the Medical University of South Carolina, noted that he entered the field by working in a rape crisis center many years ago, and that his approach is from the perspective of an epidemiologist/victimologist. "We need to improve the FBI definition of 'rape' because it is born from the 1930's view that no penis in the vagina means no rape," he said. He observed, too, that we have been too narrowly focused by looking at information only from our individual perspectives as sociologists and criminologists and we need to view these issues across disciplines, echoing a point made by Bethany Backes of NIJ. Then, he said, comes the question of, "What do I do with the data after I have it? We are good at researching," he explained, "but not good at relating that information to others." He added that more research is needed on attitudes toward sexual assault.

Cat Fribley, Resource Sharing Project Coordinator, Iowa Coalition Against Sexual Assault

Ms. Fribley, of the Resource Sharing Project at the Iowa Coalition Against Sexual Assault, noted the chilling effect the media has on rape victims, saying that there needs to be more of a focus on making victims' lives better after they have endured the initial violence and later attacks on their characters, reputations, and psyches. She said the layers of trauma faced by sexual assault victims are more in line with that of war survivors, and that research on post-traumatic stress disorder coming out of the Veterans Administration is worthy of consideration for appropriate responses to survivors of sexual violence. "We need to look at the neurobiology of trauma. Currently, there is a gap between neurobiology and the statistics," she said. Ms. Fribley went on to argue for more focus on offender data, mentioning that the relentless focus on victims and their characteristics and behaviors takes scrutiny off the offenders. She also pressed for a closer examination of both advocate efficacy and prosecutorial discretion.

Discussion

In the discussion segment, Dr. Walter S. DeKeseredy agreed that we need close examination of perpetrators: "Why do they do what they do and keep doing it?" He pointed out that Internet pornography is an $87 billion industry and is powerful in shaping views on sex and violence. "We have looked at these problems from a narrow scope for way too long, and we are losing the communication battle," he said, adding that we need to do a better job of translating these stories in our field.

Dr. Kilpatrick remarked that, "things evolve, and *we* need to as well. We need a blend of social science that we can push to the media and have your grandmother understand." When that

---

happens, he said, we can be effective in taking sexual assault cases to law enforcement, prosecutors, and juries.

When one participant asked about how to get the NIBRS data to the media, Dr. Snyder pointed out that NIBRS is simply a software program and can be accessed without much difficulty. There was a call among the group members to get the NIBRS data out in media blasts that are short and easy to comprehend.

Dr. Courtney E. Ahrens, associate professor at California State University, Long Beach, then agreed with an earlier point made that there are too many information "silos" and that there needs to be a central information repository.

Continuing the discussion of research gaps, Dr. Callie Rennison, associate professor at the University of Colorado at Denver, suggested that when one has a question about a specific piece of research, why not simply call authors and pose it directly?

Dr. DeKeseredy later asked about getting effective data in the university setting so that school presidents can put it to good use and prevent sexual violence on campuses. Claudia Bayliff, Project Attorney with the National Judicial Education Program – Legal Momentum, then asked whether translational ability should be a required element of proposal funding.

When Judge Carbon again noted the campus safety summit being hosted in October, Dr. DeKeseredy remarked that schools want funding, but no school wants to be stuck with the "Date Rape University" tag.

Working Lunch

Accurately Presenting Sexual Violence and Victimization in Research

Courtney E. Ahrens, Ph.D., Associate Professor of Psychology, California State University, Long Beach

Anne K. Ream, Survivor, Writer, and Founder, Voices and Faces Project

Karen D. Carroll, Survivor and Associate Director, Bronx SART

During lunch, Dr. Ahrens gave a short presentation on quantitative and qualitative analysis, making the point that both are needed to generate rich and useful information on sexual assault. Elements of a survivor's story are critical to whether the victim will report the assault, police will act effectively, prosecutors will carry a case forward, and a jury will convict the defendant, she said, noting that stories provide context. She then went on to introduce Anne K. Ream, founder and creative director of the Voices and Faces Project, and Karen D. Carroll, associate director of the Bronx SART.

Both Ms. Ream and Ms. Carroll are rape survivors whose perpetrators were convicted, but their stories are very different. Ms. Carroll told of being raped by her estranged husband, and Ms.

This document is intended to reflect the conversation among roundtable participants and does not necessarily reflect the opinions of the United States Department of Justice.

February 2012 | Page 16 of 26

Ream shared her story of rape by a stranger who entered her apartment building. Both articulated a fear that they would die if they did not do what their attackers demanded of them, and both described their determination to stay alive through their assaults. "During all of the fear and agony is when I wanted to live most," Ms. Ream said. "In a moment of terror, you are transformed outside of yourself." Ms. Carroll and Ms. Ream described the aftermath of their assaults, including responses from law enforcement, hospital personnel, prosecutors, and family and friends. Ms. Carroll, herself an emergency room nurse at the time, recounted having gone to a different hospital from the one where she worked so she would not know the staff, and the staff would not know her. She described how the doctor who performed her medical forensic exam "opened up the rape kit and began to read the instructions." Her experience in receiving poor medical forensic care, she explained, led to her decision to pursue forensic nursing.

"I've been raped," Ms. Ream told her mother after the incident. "All you are is broken." She recalled that "all of a sudden, I went from being Anne to being known as a 'witness.'" Counseling that "survivors need to be able to express it all, and checking a box on a survey form won't do it for them," she explained that "the need for effective storytelling is what drives me in helping other victims tell their stories. How to marry the trauma with the stories about rebuilding our lives is paramount." Ms. Ream said that her Voices and Faces Web site features the stories of 300 women and men who have provided detailed responses to questions about rape and its impact on their lives. She explained that these stories help rebuild lives and help the broader public understand the personal impact of violence.

Afternoon Session

Research on Sexual Violence: Issues in Reporting, Law Enforcement Response, and SANE-SART

Kimberly A. Lonsway, Ph.D., Research Director, End Violence Against Women International

Dr. Kimberly A. Lonsway of End Violence Against Women International, said that we need to have a better sense of what happens to sexual assault cases in the criminal justice system from the beginning point of reporting to police through the final end point of conviction and incarceration. When studies begin at the point of prosecution, most of the attrition has already taken place and it provides a misleading picture of what has happened. We also need to study the intermediate steps of an investigation and prosecution that represent additional points of attrition – most studies focus only on the obvious attrition points of arrest and prosecution. Yet in between there are a number of decisions made by police and prosecutors that determine which cases move forward and which ones do not – for example, the decision to interview the suspect, to locate and interview witnesses, to collect certain evidence. Given research findings on the frequency of re-perpetration, an important decision must be made to seek out any additional victims who might have been sexually assaulted by the same suspect. She said we need real attrition data that pieces everything together because "these cases do not involve one-time actors, and we need to start looking for other victims."

Rebecca Campbell, Ph.D., Professor of Community Psychology and Program Evaluation, Michigan State University

Dr. Rebecca Campbell of Michigan State University said that the first phase of the investigation is a key area for further research because differences in how victims convey their experiences may have a profound impact on case outcomes. What and how a victim discloses influences the law enforcement response, and even cases with substantial evidence may not be taken by prosecutors if the victim's credibility is at all vulnerable. It is critical to understand why some cases are seen through adjudication and sentencing while others do not make it past the initial police report.

James P. Markey, Detective Sergeant, Phoenix (AZ) Police Department

James P. Markey, Detective Sergeant, Phoenix (AZ) Police Department, remarked that "your research is the donut of law enforcement." He asked participants to "please continue to feed us more and more," drawing laughter.

Sgt. Markey then noted that the reality of large caseloads means that some police departments have to "triage" rape cases because they simply don't have the fiscal resources and personnel to tackle them all. "So, right away a decision is made that may impact what cases go forward and what cases fall away." He suggested that there needs to be an analysis of what is an acceptable caseload for an investigator, noting that in addition to investigating, taking interviews and gathering crime scene evidence, administrative tasks can account for as much as 60 percent of an investigator's time.

Discussion

Ms. Fribley said she understood this dilemma and noted that this lack of resources makes it more important for advocates to have a solid rapport with police, which may lead to better outcomes for victims. Professor Kilpatrick agreed that municipal and state resources are low and that sex assault cases are triaged. This reality may lead to law enforcement choosing the cases that are easiest to close and push forward to prosecution.

Dr. William M. Green, clinical professor with the Department of Emergency Medicine, University of California Davis Health System, observed that the television show CSI has created a "powerful" phenomenon where juries expect to see all of the evidence in a case presented neatly for resolution. Such TV shows feed unrealistic expectations, and survivors, researchers, and prosecutors need to reclaim the territory seized by CSI, he said. At the same time, Sgt. Markey said, the CSI effect can be positive when there is a DNA match in the rape case and the defendant knows the "game is up" and he will be convicted based on that evidence.

Research on Sexual Violence: Prosecution, Adjudication, and Sentencing

Cassia C. Spohn, Ph.D., Professor, Arizona State University

Dr. Cassia C. Spohn of Arizona State University discussed the practice by which police have discretion to clear cases by "exceptional means," essentially erasing sexual assaults from the books without ever resolving them. She noted that few assault cases even make it to the sentencing stage, and that this practice just worsens the attrition. She said that one of the unintended consequences of this practice is that perpetrators escape being captured or charged, no DNA testing is ever done on them, and there is no arrest record. So, not only are victims harmed, but these perpetrators are often allowed to become serial rapists. However, she noted, the law in California now requires that a suspect's DNA be taken in all felony cases, and that the change may make a difference in tracking down rapists even if they initially escape prosecution due to the "exceptional means" process. Still, she thinks that this is a questionable practice because it gives police and prosecutors too much authority to dodge cases they deem hard to win and it never counts against the prosecutor's win-loss record.

"If you file the dog, you walk the dog," Professor Spohn said, referring to the familiar saying of prosecutors in Los Angeles. Thus, prosecutors in Los Angeles heavily scrutinize cases before they bring them, she said.

Jennifer G. Long, Director, AEquitas, Washington, DC

Attorney Jennifer Long, director of AEquitas, said that Dr. Spohn's work is important, and as a former prosecutor, she finds this practice "horrible" and "unethical." She suggested that prosecutors need to think less about their personal careers and more about community safety. "There is a myth about offenders, and when one comes into court and does not appear as menacing as we might perceive a rapist to be, that creates problems for prosecutors," she added.

Hon. Jerry J. Bowles, Circuit Judge, Family Court, Jefferson County, KY

Judge Jerry J. Bowles, Circuit Judge of the family court in Jefferson County, Kentucky, noted that while prosecutors seek to eliminate the problem cases in this gatekeeper role, the prosecutor's power is too broad because it permits assumptions to be made about a victim's personal habits (e.g., drug use), character (e.g., sexual history), and other aspects that have nothing to do with the assault. This type of discretion is biased and is deeply entrenched, said Judge Bowles. And it does not simply occur in a vacuum.

Judge Bowles mentioned an analogy he uses often in training judges and others across the country, an experience that anyone can readily understand:

> Think of visiting a funeral home upon the death of a friend or family member. Some guests will cry; others will laugh and tell jokes, remembering the good

---

times; others will simply smile and embrace friends in a gesture of support; others will shut their eyes and hold their feelings close. Despite how vastly different these reactions are, no one leaves the funeral home doubting that someone died.

Discussion

Anne Ream noted that there is a serious problem with some prosecutors believing that false reporting of rape is rampant. Ms. Ream asked: "Are prosecutors and judges driving the culture, or are they driven by the culture? We have to ask ourselves what we are going to do to turn this situation around and where is our political courage?" she said.

Dr. Ahrens suggested a closer look how decisions are made regarding the judicial administration of these cases. She cited one case where a specialized court for sexual assaults was shut down after "someone" decided that sex crimes cases were no longer a top priority. The court was later made a court for handling drug cases and then closed down altogether.

Summation of the Day and Concluding Remarks

Kristina Rose, Deputy Director of NIJ, outlined some of the main themes from the first day of discussion:

- ▶ Heavy discussion of dissemination of information, translating information across fields, sexual assault definitions, and victim behaviors.

- ▶ Qualitative and quantitative research are both critical to providing rich and relevant information about sexual violence.

- ▶ Focus on perpetrators.
  - – Study them better because they often commit the same crime over and over.
  - – Large victim pools and DNA evidence can help identify offenders.

- ▶ Combining strong numerical data with effective storytelling will give us a comprehensive picture of sexual violence and its impact.

- ▶ Power of NIBRS data to give practitioners, policymakers, and the public useful information about sexual violence.

- ▶ Research questions that explore:
  - – How to apply surveys to a community that has no word for "rape"
  - – Getting away from yes/no questions
  - – The impact of trauma
  - – Prosecutorial discretion
  - – Acceptable sexual assault caseloads for investigators
  - – Critical factors that lead to a successful outcome

- Identifying the wide range of "normal" victim behaviors
▶ Drive home the message that, just like other tragedies, rape is a real and serious crime, and perpetrators—not victims—should be the subjects of scrutiny.
▶ In a moment of terror, you are transformed outside of yourself.
- Need to account for the profound and long-term impact of rape.

Day Two, Friday, September 9, 2011

Morning Discussion

Lynn Rosenthal, White House Advisor on Violence Against Women, thanked the Department of Justice leaders for convening the roundtable discussion and working tirelessly to end violence against women. She noted the importance of the upcoming 17th anniversary of the Violence Against Women Act (VAWA) and said that the Obama Administration, which held the first White House roundtable on sexual assault last year, is at the forefront on this issue. Ms. Rosenthal stated that Vice President Biden has been on top of this issue for almost two decades and was a key supporter of this important law long ago. She added that important strides are being made to end sexual violence and told the audience that "none of this would be possible without your work."

Reflections on Yesterday: What Was Most Relevant, and What Important Ideas or Questions Did We Miss?

Dr. Kilpatrick noted the importance of applying broad concepts to actual practice. He suggested that it is important to measure attitudes over time to see if views really change, and there needs to be a study that can do this.

Dr. Sharon Murphy, assistant professor in the University of New Hampshire Social Work Department, noted that many parts of the country operate differently and that the "exceptional clearances" practice, while prolific in Los Angeles, may not apply in other areas of the country. Further, she said, the decision to have the rape kit tested is not always the sole decision of the prosecutor. She also pointed out that obtaining statistical information from law enforcement and prosecutors is not an easy matter in many jurisdictions.

Drawing from Dr. Kilpatrick's point on measuring community attitudes, another participant noted that community attitudes on college campuses need to be studied closely. On that point, Ms. Ream said that attitudes cannot be assessed without also looking at the media and how rape and sexual assaults are treated by news outlets. Dr. Sujata Warrier, director of the New York City Program, NYS Office for the Prevention of Domestic Violence, said the notion of "community" needs to be viewed in a more complex way because a police officer or health care practitioner is not always the first person to whom victims disclose sexual assault, particularly in marginalized communities. In some communities, she noted, that person may be a priest, pastor, or some other figure.

Ms. Fribley noted that in focusing on sexual violence against women, it is important not to omit children, the elderly, the mentally ill, and other marginalized people.

Dissemination and Use of Sexual Violence Research in the Criminal Justice System—Improving Research-to-Practice and Effectively Translating Research for Practice

Claire M. Renzetti, Ph.D., Judi Conway Patton Endowed Chair and Professor of Sociology, University of Kentucky

Dr. Renzetti noted that violence against women research is translational by nature. Researchers studying violence against women do not conduct studies simply to satisfy intellectual curiosity; research is purpose-driven in that we want our research to be used or applied to improve services, help victims, and understand offenders. But there is often a disconnect between conducting purpose-driven research and making the findings accessible to practitioners. Book publishers are more aware of this problem than journal editors and encourage authors to make their work more accessible to nonacademic audiences. Dr. Renzetti speculated that part of the difficulty is the way students are trained to write in graduate school and as junior faculty; they learn a formulaic style that can be seen in nearly all journal articles. Consequently, Dr. Renzetti suggested that researchers reconsider how graduate students and junior faculty are trained, not only in terms of writing style, but also to encourage them to include the policy and practice implications of their research in their book and journal manuscripts. Both journal editors and peer reviewers need to value this as well. She also emphasized the need to change the value structure that underlies, tenure, promotion, and merit review within disciplines, departments, and universities, so that researchers pay more than mere lip service to interdisciplinarity and collaboration. Senior faculty, department chairs, and deans must reward interdisciplinary work and collaborations between researchers and practitioners, which is currently not the case in many academic settings.

Jolene Hernon, Director, Office of Communications, National Institute of Justice

Ms. Jolene Hernon, director of the Office of Communications at NIJ, stressed that the audience should consider writing from a busy decisionmaker's perspective who has time to read only about 20 lines. Impactful statements need to be short. It should not take 250 pages to convey a message. The message should be made simple. It should have a beginning, middle and end, like any good story. Ms. Hernon also remarked that blogs are getting more credibility, and it is clear that there is a shift underway in how people obtain information. Thus, writing styles must account for the formats through which information is presented.

Claudia J. Bayliff, J.D., Project Attorney, National Judicial Education Program –
Legal Momentum, Falls Church, VA

Ms. Claudia J. Bayliff, Project Attorney, National Judicial Education Program – Legal Momentum, insisted that official statistics be stated correctly. But she acknowledged that this would be difficult because using definitions other than those in the UCR can send the rape and sexual assault numbers off the charts, creating a communications nightmare and leading to political backlash. She suggested that participants' websites need to be connected and share consistent messages. "Have a good answer to the top 25 'bonehead' questions that you get asked because they come up all the time," Ms. Bayliff said. "Why not have solid, consistent answers when we already know the questions?" She suggested partnering with the military on some of these issues because, for example, the United States Air Force deals with sexual assaults system wide.

Ms. Bayliff also cautioned about language choice in writing. We talk about rapists "having sex with" victims and use the word "accuser," she noted. We also say the rape "occurred," which she finds puzzling: "Earthquakes occur, but rape is intentionally done."

Researcher-Practitioner Teams

Participants broke into small groups to identify the most pressing research questions or topics and describe how results may be useful for policy and practice.

Team One Topic: General Populations' Attitudes Regarding Rape and Sexual Assault

Participants identified the need to better understand public perceptions of sexual violence as an urgent priority, and then use those findings as the basis for new efforts to change attitudes and prevent sexual violence. Strategies included:

- ► Conduct a study of the general population's perceptions of sexual violence.
- ► Conduct longitudinal research over five years.
- ► Include a survivor-focused multimedia response.
- ► Use results of a study of attitudes about sexual violence to develop an effective messaging campaign.

Team Two Topic: Attitudes on Rape/Sexual Assault in Five Major Markets

Participants in this group suggested that existing national surveys could be supplemented with sections that would generate more detailed data on sexual violence. Strategies included:

- ► Addend the National Crime Victimization Survey (NCVS) sections on rape and sexual assault to include more detailed measurements in five metropolitan areas, e.g., New York, New Jersey, Phoenix, Miami, and Dallas, to get a more comprehensive picture of sexual violence and the criminal justice response.

This document is intended to reflect the conversation among roundtable participants and does not necessarily reflect the opinions of the United States Department of Justice.

- Piggyback on the upcoming BJS study on the measurement of rape in five communities, and examine how many cases are reported, attrition, attitudes, and the media.

- Conduct a comprehensive study on attitudes within the criminal justice system and the media.

Team Three Topic: Forensic Medical Exams: Advantages and Disadvantages

This team urged for partnerships among researchers and practitioners—and among federal agencies—to study the long-term effects of sexual violence. Additionally, participants recommended further research on the benefits and drawbacks of the medical forensic exam. The strategies they identified were:

- Ask what the benefits of the medical forensic exam are to the individual and the criminal justice system.

- Look at the advantages and disadvantages of the medical forensic exam, to determine:

  - What practices, techniques, and technologies are effective?

  - What are the benefits for survivors and for the criminal justice system? The medical forensic exam adds trauma onto trauma for victims, yet often times the sexual assault kit is never processed. How do the benefits and the drawbacks of undergoing an exam compare for survivors?

- Forge new partnerships with the CDC and Substance Abuse and Mental Health Services Administration (SAMHSA) and the criminal justice system and examine long-term health impacts of sexual violence.

- Look at health effects at individual and community levels.

Team Four Topic: Using Research to Improve the First Response System

This team emphasized the critical effect that the first response to sexual violence can have on victims' experiences and case outcomes. Strategies included:

- Examine what components of a first response system are necessary and useful.

- Ask what might lead to more help-seeking behaviors; what are the exam outcomes; what can be done more effectively; and what can be eliminated.

- Organize within disciplines and collaborate.

Team Five Topic: Addressing Multiple Needs and Multiple Victimizations Using a Direct Advocacy Strategy

Participants highlighted the need among advocates, law enforcement, attorneys, and others to respond effectively to survivors who have been victimized more than once and/or in multiple ways. These survivors often have complex needs, and practitioners can sometimes feel ill-equipped to help them. Strategies included:

- ▶ Examine multiple needs and multiple victimizations and include a study on advocacy as a first response.

- ▶ Examine what improves quality of life for survivors, particularly for those who do not report to law enforcement.

Team Six Topic: Law Enforcement Efficiency/Capability

Participants in this group focused on the need to study organizational barriers to investigating sexual assaults and effective approaches to crime control and prevention. Strategies included:

- ▶ Conduct a study to determine an acceptable caseload for detectives, given that police departments are under severe fiscal and personnel constraints.

- ▶ Ask whether special victims units are effective, especially given that they are often the first units to be trimmed in budget cuts.

- ▶ Examine more crime control and safety measures.

- ▶ Examine whether a multidimensional model is more effective.

- ▶ Conduct more research on serial offenders, including prevention strategies that address serial offenders.

Team Seven Topic: Prosecution Attitudes and Practices

Participants in this group also urged for research on prosecutors' and the general public's attitudes toward sexual violence. They called for research on if and how social media, video games, and pornography influence or change an individual's perceptions of sexual violence. Strategies included:

- ▶ Design studies looking at changes in attitudes about sexual assault.

- ▶ Examine how pornography and video game violence spill into mainstream media, and what effect, if any, this has on attitudes about sexual violence.

- ▶ Examine effects of social media on sexual violence: its perpetration, responses to it, and attitudes surrounding it.

Concluding Remarks and Next Steps

Kristina Rose of NIJ thanked all of her colleagues and counterparts for organizing the meeting and said this precedent makes an effective footprint for future collaboration and leveraging of information. She noted that a new office at NIJ had been created, the Office of Research Partnerships, and that she was overseeing the transition and working to ensure that research information is widely disseminated and that research dollars go farther.

This document is intended to reflect the conversation among roundtable participants and does not necessarily reflect the opinions of the United States Department of Justice.

February 2012 | Page 25 of 26

Director Carbon of OVW thanked Ms. Rose for her work on this meeting and thanked the participants for attending. Director Carbon also thanked Anne Ream and Karen Carroll for sharing their stories with the group. "You are the face and voices of what we do," she told them. Director Carbon and the other Federal partners said that the information from this meeting would be shared with the White House and the Attorney General's office. She also again noted the upcoming summit on campus safety and said that college campuses are an important forum where the message on rape and sexual violence can be reshaped. "We must win this communications battle," she said.

The meeting was adjourned.

APPENDIX A:

PARTICIPANT LIST

NIJ
National Institute of Justice

**Sexual Violence
Research Roundtable**

Arlington, VA   September 8–9, 2011

OVW
Office on Violence Against Women

PARTICIPANT LIST

Courtney E. Ahrens, Ph.D.
Associate Professor
California State University at Long Beach
Department of Psychology

Kathleen C. Basile, Ph.D.
Lead Behavioral Scientist
Centers for Disease Control and Prevention
Division of Violence Prevention

Claudia J. Bayliff, M.A., J.D.
Project Attorney
National Judicial Education Program

Eve Birge
Education Program Specialist
Office of Safe and Drug Free Schools
U.S. Department of Education

Jerry J. Bowles
Judge
Circuit Court
Louisville, KY

Rebecca Campbell, Ph.D.
Professor of Psychology
Michigan State University

Karen D. Carroll
Associate Director
Bronx SART

Kim J. Day, R.N., SANE-A, SANE-P
SAFE Technical Assistance Coordinator
International Association of Forensic Nurses

Walter S. DeKeseredy, Ph.D.
Professor of Criminology
University of Ontario Institute of Technology

Cat Fribley
RSP Coordinator
Iowa Coalition Against Sexual Assault

William M. Green, M.D.
Clinical Professor
Department of Emergency Medicine
UC Davis Health System

Monika Johnson Hostler
Executive Director
North Carolina Coalition Against Sexual Assault

Marylouise Kelley, Ph.D.
Director
Family Violence Prevention & Services Program
FYSB/ACYF/HHS

Dean Kilpatrick, Ph.D.
Distinguished University Professor of Clinical Psychology
Medical University of South Carolina
Department of Psychiatry & Behavioral Sciences
National Crime Victims Research
     & Treatment Center

Christopher Krebs, Ph.D.
Senior Research Social Scientist
Crime, Violence, and Justice Research
RTI International

T.K. Logan, Ph.D.
Professor
University of Kentucky
College of Medicine

Jennifer G. Long
Director
AEquitas

Kimberly A. Lonsway, Ph.D.
Research Director
End Violence Against Women International

Jim P. Markey
Detective Sergeant
Phoenix Police Department

Sharon Murphy, Ph.D., ACSW
Assistant Professor
University of New Hampshire
Social Work Department

Anne K. Ream
Founder and Creative Director
Voices and Faces Project

Callie Marie Rennison, Ph.D.
Associate Professor
University of Colorado at Denver
School of Public Affairs

Claire M. Renzetti, Ph.D.
Judi Conway Patton Endowed Chair
    & Professor of Sociology
University of Kentucky
Center for Research on Violence Against Women
    & Department of Sociology

Cassia C. Spohn, Ph.D.
Professor
Arizona State University
School of Criminology and Criminal Justice

Sujata Warrier, Ph.D.
Director, New York City Program
NYS Office for the Prevention of Domestic Violence

U.S. Department of Justice

Bernard Auchter
Senior Social Science Analyst
National Institute of Justice

Bethany L. Backes
Social Science Analyst
National Institute of Justice

Ginger Baran
Program Specialist
Office on Violence Against Women (OVW)

Michelle Andrea Brickley
Associate Director
Office on Violence Against Women

Susan B. Carbon
Director
Office on Violence Against Women

Shannan Catalano, Ph.D.
Statistician
Bureau of Justice Statistics

Christine R. Crossland
Senior Social Science Analyst
Office of Research & Evaluation
National Institute of Justice

Bea Hanson
Principal Deputy Director
Office on Violence Against Women

Jolene Hernon
Director, Office of Communications
National Institute of Justice

John Laub, Ph.D.
Director
National Institute of Justice

Kimberly A. Lopez
Program Specialist
Office on Violence Against Women

James P. Lynch, Ph.D.
Director
Bureau of Justice Statistics

Christina Murray
Management and Program Analyst
Office on Violence Against Women

Debra Murphy
Attorney-Advisor
Office of Justice Programs

Nancy Ritter
Writer-Editor
National Institute of Justice

Kristina Rose
Deputy Director
National Institute of Justice

Melissa Schmisek
Senior Grant Program Specialist
Office on Violence Against Women

Howard N. Snyder, Ph.D.
Deputy Director
Bureau of Justice Statistics

Debra Whitcomb
Visiting Fellow
Office for Victims of Crime

CSR, Incorporated

Karole Braunstein
Senior Meeting Planner
CSR, Incorporated

Esther Ivory-Shelborne
Senior Associate
CSR, Incorporated

Eric Yaeger
Notetaker
CSR, Incorporated

APPENDIX B:

AGENDA

Sexual Violence
Research Roundtable

National Institute of Justice

Arlington, VA   September 8–9, 2011   Office on Violence Against Women

AGENDA

Roundtable Purpose: To discuss the existing statistics and research on sexual violence and the criminal justice response, identify the research and evaluation gaps important to criminal justice reform, and determine productive directions for addressing these gaps.

DAY 1, Thursday, September 8

8:15–8:45 a.m.   REGISTRATION and COFFEE SERVICE

8:45–9:30 a.m.   **Welcome**

> **Lynn Rosenthal,** *White House Advisor on Violence Against Women, Office of the Vice President*
>
> **Hon. Susan B. Carbon,** *Director, Office on Violence Against Women*
>
> **John Laub,** *Director, National Institute of Justice*

> **Introduction of Attendees (Icebreaker Exercise)**
> **Overview of the Agenda for the Day**

9:30–10:30 a.m.   **Panel on Where We Stand: Statistics and Research on Sexual Violence**

> **Bureau of Justice Statistics**
> **Shannan Catalano,** *Statistician*
> **Howard N. Snyder,** *Deputy Director*

> **CDC, National Center for Injury Prevention and Control**
> **Kathleen C. Basile,** *Lead Behavioral Scientist, Division of Violence Prevention*

> **National Institute of Justice**
> **Bethany Backes,** *Social Science Analyst*

> **Discussion**

10:30–10:45 a.m.   BREAK

10:45 a.m.–12:15 p.m. **Discussion Session**

> **Statistics and Data on Sexual Violence**

> **Opening Comments**

> > **TK Logan,** *Professor, University of Kentucky*
> >
> > **Dean Kilpatrick,** *Distinguished University Professor of Clinical Psychology, Medical University of South Carolina*
> >
> > **Cat Fribley,** *RSP Coordinator, Iowa Coalition Against Sexual Assault*

12:15–1:35 p.m.   WORKING LUNCH

Panel: Accurately Presenting Sexual Violence and Victimization in Research

> **Courtney E. Ahrens,** *Associate Professor of Psychology, California State University, Long Beach*
> **Anne K. Ream,** *Survivor, Writer and Founder, Voices and Faces Project*
> **Karen D. Carroll,** *Survivor and Associate Director, Bronx SART*

1:35 p.m.–1:45 p.m.   BREAK

1:45–3:00 p.m.   **Discussion Session**

Research on Sexual Violence: Issues in Reporting, Law Enforcement Response, and SANE-SART

Opening Comments

> **Kimberly A. Lonsway,** *Research Director, End Violence Against Women International*
> **Rebecca Campbell,** *Professor of Community Psychology and Program Evaluation, Michigan State University*
> **James P. Markey,** *Detective Sergeant, Phoenix (AZ) Police Department*

3:00–3:15 p.m.   BREAK

3:15–4:30 p.m.   **Discussion Session**

Research on Sexual Violence: Prosecution, Adjudication, and Sentencing

Opening Comments

> **Cassia C. Spohn,** *Professor, Arizona State University*
> **Jennifer G. Long,** *Director, AEquitas*
> **Hon. Jerry J. Bowles,** *Circuit Judge, Family Court, Jefferson County, KY*

4:30–5:00 p.m.   **Summation of the Day and a Concluding Remarks**
                      Kristina Rose, *Deputy Director, National Institute of Justice*

Day 2, Friday, September 9

8:15–8:45 a.m.	COFFEE SERVICE

8:45–9:45 a.m.   **Reflections on Yesterday: What Was Most Relevant, and What Important Ideas or Questions Did We Miss?**

9:45–10:00 a.m.   BREAK

10:00–11:30 a.m.   **Discussion**

Dissemination and Use of Sexual Violence Research in the Criminal Justice System—Improving Research-to-Practice and Effectively Translating Research for Practice

Opening Comments

> **Claire Renzetti,** *Professor, University of Kentucky*
> **Jolene Hernon,** *Director, Office of Communications, National Institute of Justice*
> **Claudia J. Bayliff,** *Project Attorney, National Judicial Education Program*

11:30 a.m.–12:30 p.m.   Final Exercise

Researcher and Practitioner Teams List Their Most Important Research Question Needing to Be Addressed and How the Results May be Useful for Policy or Practice

Concluding Comments and Next Steps

> **Hon. Susan B. Carbon,** *Director, Office on Violence Against Women*

www.ingramcontent.com/pod-product-compliance
Lightning Source LLC
Chambersburg PA
CBHW080638290526
45790CB00007B/3118